Bonobos

by Grace Hansen

Abdo
ANIMAL FRIENDS
Kids

abdopublishing.com

Published by Abdo Kids, a division of ABDO, PO Box 398166, Minneapolis, Minnesota 55439.

Copyright © 2016 by Abdo Consulting Group, Inc. International copyrights reserved in all countries. No part of this book may be reproduced in any form without written permission from the publisher.

Printed in the United States of America, North Mankato, Minnesota.

052015

092015

 THIS BOOK CONTAINS RECYCLED MATERIALS

Photo Credits: Corbis, iStock, Minden Pictures, Science Source, Shutterstock

Production Contributors: Teddy Borth, Jennie Forsberg, Grace Hansen

Design Contributors: Laura Rask, Dorothy Toth

Library of Congress Control Number: 2014958408

Cataloging-in-Publication Data

Hansen, Grace.

 Bonobos / Grace Hansen.

   p. cm. -- (Animal friends)

 ISBN 978-1-62970-895-9

 Includes index.

 1. Bonobo--Juvenile literature.   I. Title.

 599.88--dc23

                    2014958408

Table of Contents

Bonobos

Bonobos live in Africa.

They live in the rain forest.

Bonobos look like
chimpanzees. But they
are thinner than chimps.

They have smaller heads than chimps. They also have smaller ears.

Food

Bonobos eat fruits. They eat leaves and stems. They also eat fish and insects.

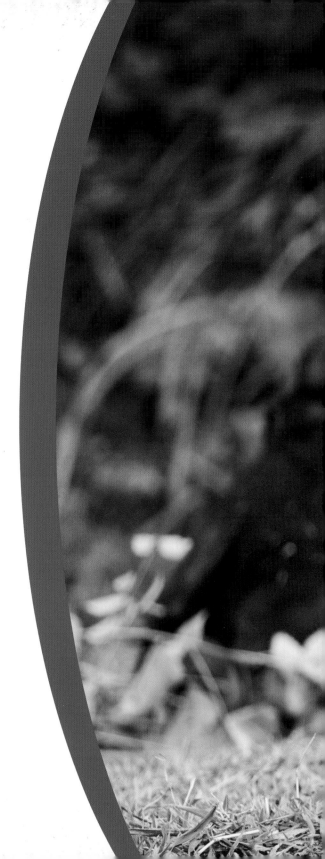

Behavior

Bonobos **rarely** fight when they are mad. They **comfort** one another instead.

Female bonobos are in charge of groups. This is **rare** for animals. Males usually lead groups.

14

Kind to All

Bonobos are peaceful. They let strangers into their areas. Other great apes do not allow this.

16

Bonobos love to share.

They share their nests.

They also share their food.

They share with their friends and families. They even share with strangers! Bonobos teach us to be kind to everyone.

More Facts

- Bonobos are very peaceful. They have never been seen killing their own kind. This is unlike other great apes.

- Sometimes male bonobos get angry. The females put a stop to any fighting. Over time, males have become less **aggressive**.

- There are few bonobos left in the wild. They are endangered. It is important that humans **protect** them.

Glossary

aggressive – ready and willing to fight.

comfort – to cause someone to feel less upset or scared.

protect – to keep safe from harm.

rare – not usual.

23

Index

abdokids.com

Use this code to log on to abdokids.com and access crafts, games, videos, and more!

Abdo Kids Code:
ABK8959